Boat

Also by Christopher Merrill

Poetry

Workbook

Fevers & Tides

Watch Fire

7 Poets, 4 Days, 1 Poem (collaborative poem with Marvin Bell, István László Geher, Ksenia Golubovich, Simone Inguanez, Tomaž Šalamun, and Dean Young)

Necessities

Translations

Anxious Moments, prose poems by Aleš Debeljak (translated with the author)

The City and the Child, poems by Aleš Debeljak (translated with the author)

Even Birds Leave the World: Selected Poems of Ji-woo Hwang
(translated with Won-Chung Kim)

Because of the Rain: A Selection of Korean Zen Poems
(translated with Won-Chung Kim)

Scale and Stairs: Selected Poems of Heeduk Ra (translated with Won-Chung Kim)

Translucency: Selected Poems of Chankyung Sung (translated with Won-Chung Kim)

The Growth of a Shadow: Selected Poems of Taejoon Moon (translated with Won-Chung Kim)

Essays and literary journalism

The Grass of Another Country: A Journey Through the World of Soccer

The Old Bridge: The Third Balkan War and the Age of the Refugee

The Forest of Speaking Trees: An Essay on Poetry

Your Final Pleasure: An Essay on Reading

Only the Nails Remain: Scenes from the Balkan Wars

Things of the Hidden God: Journey to the Holy Mountain

The Tree of the Doves: Ceremony, Expedition, War

Edited volumes

Outcroppings: John McPhee in the West

The Forgotten Language: Contemporary Poets and Nature

From the Faraway Nearby: Georgia O'Keeffe as Icon (with Ellen Bradbury)

What Will Suffice: Contemporary American Poets on the Art of Poetry
(with Christopher Buckley)

The Way to the Salt Marsh: A John Hay Reader

The Four Questions of Melancholy: New and Selected Poems of Tomaž Šalamun

The New Symposium: Poets and Writers on What We Hold in Common
(with Nataša Ďurovičová)

B O A T

CHRISTOPHER MERRILL

POEMS

TUPELO PRESS
NORTH ADAMS, MASSACHUSETTS

Library of Congress Cataloging-in-Publication Data
Merrill, Christopher.
[Poems. Selections]
Boat : Poems / Christopher Merrill. -- First edition.
    pages cm
Includes bibliographical references.
ISBN 978-1-936797-38-7 (paperback original : alk. paper)
I. Title.
PS3563.E74517A6 2013
811'.54--dc23

2013034371

First edition: October 2013.

Cover and text designed by Bill Kuch.
Cover art: Gabriela Vainsencher, *"El Barco, for Jeffrey"* (detail), 2013. Sumi ink
on paper. Used courtesy of the artist (http://gabrielavainsencher.com/).

Tupelo Press
P.O. Box 1767
243 Union Street, Eclipse Mill, Loft 305
North Adams, Massachusetts 01247
Telephone: (413) 664–9611 / Fax: (413) 664–9711
editor@tupelopress.org / www.tupelopress.org

Tupelo Press is an award-winning independent literary press that publishes
fine fiction, nonfiction, and poetry in books that are a joy to hold as well as
read. Tupelo Press is a registered 501(c)3 nonprofit organization, and we rely on
public support to carry out our mission of publishing extraordinary work that
may be outside the realm of large commercial publishers. Financial donations
are welcome and are tax deductible.

for my teachers

Contents

I

II

III

IV

Racine: What's that?
Matty: A gazebo.
Racine: No, out there.
Matty: Boat house.
Racine: What is in there?
Matty: Boat.

— *Body Heat* (1981)

I

The Ground Swell

arriving from another continent
to tilt the buoy toward the shirtless sailors
bewildered by the sudden rise of water
and, reclining on the bow, the lovers
who hope the afternoon will never end,
leaves the outrigger in a trough, leaning
shoreward, on the same axis as the buoy,
with its mast bisecting a line of high thin clouds
laid like paving stones on the blue altar
of the sky, in a V that points beyond the canvas,
where the wave travels on to meet the shore
and the sunbathers lolling on the sand,
the fisherman mending his nets, the actress
climbing a palm tree to escape the crowd
of autograph seekers and paparazzi
positioning themselves along the beach
and hotel balcony, the tourist boat
departing for a blasted coral reef,
the lifeguards, waiters, and bartenders scanning
the clouds on the horizon for a sign
that their way of life is coming to an end—
guns oiled and ready, the ramparts fortified,
an editor retrieving from the morgue
the words of the wit who vanished in the desert:
War, said the Gringo in Mexico, *is God's way
of teaching Americans geography.*

—after the painting by Edward Hopper (1939)

Notes for a Journey to the Interior

The Window

The paint sealing the window turned to dust
Before they tried to open it. No luck.
And no one ever looked outside again.
The files were loaded on a boat, the militia
Cordoned off the square, the weatherman
Predicted forty days and nights of rain.
Thank God the window wouldn't open.

The Storm

Lightning, and the boy counting with his fingers,
And the dog whimpering under the bed—
The monk said, *You must die to everything
Before your body dies* . . . Rumble of thunder,
Rain in the eaves. Rejoice, rejoice! No one
Will hear the lover's argument, when the wind
In the ravine sweeps up the leaves of the diseased
Oak and lifts the skin sloughed off by the snake
The dog uncovered and the boy won't catch.

The Tent

The tables spun in the white tent, which rose
Into the branches of the dying oak
Above the flooding river: twelve moons revolving
Around the guests who left before the speeches
In which the town fathers reckoned our losses—
The bridge and cemetery; houses, farms,
And towers; the distance from this world to the next.

The boat to take us to higher ground was ready
For boarding. No room for the other guests.

The Sideshow

A stage with seven empty chairs and the flag
Of an imperial army on the retreat—
The gunmen in the audience will take
No hostages until the curtain rises,
The actors call off their strike, and the director,
Searching the crowd for the wife of his best friend,
Wraps himself in the flag and cries, *Lights! Action!*

The Fan

The fan spins in the citadel, lifting
The edges of the map on which they drew
Plans for their next attack. The aides-de-camp
Collect the nameplates, briefing books, and pencils.
The steward counts the silver once again.
And the note-taker gathering his papers
Tries to recall the exact words of the generals
Demoted for the timing of their warning
Against the occupation of a land
Their surveyors could not accurately appraise.
The fan spins in the dark. No one imagined
Such a departure. No one ever does.

The Funeral

A pair of soldiers in dress uniform
Smoking outside the church, with a white hearse
Blocking the fire hydrant and in the sky

Bald eagles wheeling toward the freezing river
Thick with dead fish and a new manuscript
The scribe was up all night repaginating.

The Bone

The urn remains on the widow's mantelpiece
As a rebuke to the inquisitive—
Her priest, her children, her insurance agent.
At dusk she lights the gas fire in the grate
And draws the curtains on an argument
Unfinished at his death: ice in the bird bath;
A pair of apple trees with shriveled leaves;
The hole the dog dug by the fence; and the bone
It buried and dug up. *Drop it! Good dog!*

Inland

The incense burning in the oyster shell
Next to the cup of pencils on the desk
Carries no prayers to God, only petitions
To a bank manager and a brunette
Who thought the word for *sea* was everywhere
The same, in Indonesia as in England,
On peninsulas and archipelagoes:
A word that flows through caves and crevices,
And fills the coffers of the rich, and draws
No distinction between the living and the dead.

The sweet smoke swirls above the man at prayer
Who wishes to reverse his business losses,
Redeem his move to the interior,
And resurrect the night a woman threw
Her wedding ring into the surf, believing
His drunken promises to follow her
To the ends of the earth, if not the afterlife.
The fragrance in the air belongs to whom?
Between the auditors and the audited—
This is where he waits for her, for God.

Matins

Birdsong in the dying oaks, and ribbons of fog laid on the fields and river, and in the grey light of dawn a trucker grinding gears on the hill outside of town.

Arising from sleep, the monks chant, *we fall down before thee, O Blessed God . . .*

I consult a field guide to a land that I have never visited, the flora and fauna are stranger than anyone might imagine, each day the desire to be cleansed of sin increases.

If memory lies behind a mountain range that catches the rain before it reaches the desert; if memory is surveyed in the same fashion by the adventurous and the lost; if memory is the only route to the interior . . .

Thus the sun beating down on the lumberyard, on my first day of work, as I heaved bags of cement onto pickup trucks at the loading dock.

It was too humid to breathe deeply, and when my T-shirt was soaked I stopped sweating, which amused the foreman who had hired me for the summer as a favor to my father, the new bank president from the North.

You could count on one hand the whites working there—the chain-smoking foreman, the farmer slowed by a stroke, the new recruit to the Klan, the driver who filled the paper cup on his dashboard with tobacco juice—among scores of blacks earning $3.20 an hour.

Men like Charlie Ed, who tucked a flask of vodka in his pants before he drove his forklift off the loading dock, shattering hundreds of dollars worth of sheetrock.

And blue-capped Sydney with leukemia, giving orders from atop a stack of palettes. And Clarence, a swivel-hipped, honey-voiced sawyer who had served time for murder. And Joe, who drove without a license, stopping every hour for a beer; at the end of the day he eased the flatbed into the loading dock, as if to take a seat at the counter.

A family friend arranged a blind date for me with a girl from Sweet Briar who praised her purity throughout dinner, then threw her arms around me on the way home.

On our second date she asked me how work had gone with the sawmill niggers.

Don't they smell different? she said, smoothing her hands down her yellow dress.

I wish I could say that we never went out again, but I had no other friends in Raleigh.

Forgive me, Charlie Ed and Sydney, Clarence and Joe, and all the men who taught me the virtue of holding my tongue.

And forgive me, Ashley, for my confusion and clumsiness, which have hardly diminished in the years since we groped for each other in the dark.

Nor did I learn until much later about the death threats that my father had received after laying off hundreds of employees.

The branch manager, for example, who opened the vault every Friday for an office party.

And the lawyer who wanted to become a woman—my father advised him to move to San Francisco: Raleigh wasn't ready for *that,* he explained.

And otherwise decent men and women who fell victim to a raft of bad loans brought on by the oil crisis—i.e., to decisions that in retrospect appeared foolish.

As my mother would say of our move to Raleigh: *the worst decision of our marriage.*

But my father made a good business out of salvaging failed banks, each of which he sold to a larger bank and moved on—a lesson in economics that I could not grasp.

The guitar was no less mystifying, though I went to the mall once a week to take lessons from a studio musician, who taught me the chords to "A Peaceful, Easy Feeling," a state of mind that my strumming failed to inspire in anybody.

Carelessness nearly cost me my life twice that summer—once on the interstate, when I fell asleep listening to George Harrison on the eight-track and drifted into the median, and once at a bluegrass festival in Danville, Virginia, the last capital of the Confederacy.

I was walking toward the music on a road in the woods when a motorcyclist weaving in and out of the crowd lost control and skidded into me.

Someone helped me into a van, which drove slowly enough for the man in the passenger seat to sell hashish and LSD out the window.

I lost consciousness in the ambulance, and woke in the hospital when orderlies laid me on a gurney next to an overdose victim.

A state trooper was tugging the man's ponytail, saying, *Wake up. You're under arrest.*

While the monks chanted, *Do thou enlighten my understanding and my heart, and open my lips, that I may sing of thee, O Holy Trinity.*

Politics

The girl is playing dress-up, and the boy
Hides in the fort he dug around the dogwood,
Examining the sandwich board his neighbor
Sliced up with a knife—the photographs
Cut out of *Look* and *Life,* then taped below
The slogans printed (aslant) in large block letters:
GOLDWATER *64* and PUT YOUR MONEY
WHERE YOUR FAITH IS. He doesn't understand
What the words shredded by the older boy
Mean, nor what spurred this hatred for a man
His parents praise at dinner . . . From his lookout
In the woods between the neighbor's house and theirs
He sees his sister in the picture window,
Poised in a wedding dress, and the other boy
Guarding the hill he marched across all morning,
Proclaiming—in cardboard—his faith in signs
That only the adults seem to understand:
The sky is overcast. No one is safe.

———————

The boy has inventoried the bomb shelter—
Sand, cinder blocks, and rats; discarded planks
Of wood and two-by-fours; a set of hinges
And enough rusted nails to build a new
Fort in the ashes—and has surveyed the fallout
From the storm: books and cardboard boxes floating
In ankle-deep water; a burned-out light bulb
Unscrewed from the socket in the ceiling;
The warped head of his wooden tennis racket.
His sister dances on the Ping-Pong table,
Singing *Poor boy, you're bound to die,* and swings
A plastic jug of Clorox that she will drink from,

If he will wade in bare feet through the water
And, rising on his tiptoes, stick his finger
Into the empty socket. Which he does,
Against his better instincts. His eyes widen
And swirl, his body quivers, he can't let go.
His sister takes a swig, and sings, *Poor boy* . . .

———————

When the wind rises, and the burning leaves
Sail toward the neighbor's grove of Christmas trees,
The rows of noble firs and white pine seedlings
Planted the year before to supplement
His income from the bakery, apple orchard,
And boxes of honey bees by the garage,
The children watch their father raise his arms
And mutter, *Jesus Christ.* A field of flames
Is hard to turn away from, even if
Your father orders you to follow him.
So when he runs back to the house to call
The fire department—the volunteers who leave
Their farms, framing jobs, and broken sewer lines
To try to save some portion of a village
Crisscrossed by brooks—the children stay behind
To mark how fast the fire consumes the land,
How loud the hissing of the flames, how small
The baker tallying his losses looks.

Ark

Back and forth, back and forth: how she would swim
Laps in the pond carved out of stone—the polar bear
Caught on an ice floe severed from a glacier
And sold from zoo to zoo. A crowd assembled
Beyond the rusting mesh to watch her rise
Like a birch tree above the overhang,
And arc her back under the autumn sky,
And splash in the black water, and swim away.
The children on their father's shoulders shrieked.
She couldn't stop herself. Nor could I.

The snail that slept for three years had nothing on the bluebird flying upside down in the canyon of the ancient ones, circling the ruins in which we renamed the world.

Venus is the only planet that rotates clockwise. Is this why love creates its own measure of time—outside time? And why does it turn counter?

The cat in heat screams through the night, upsets the candles on the table, wakes the children.

If butterflies taste with their feet, and the eye of the ostrich is bigger than its brain, surely we can devise new ways to taste and see.

Lolita, the myna bird called at dusk, when I hurried through the aviary with the one who would betray me again before the cock crowed.

There is no other way to say this: the cow you led up the stairs will not come down.

Oak trees produce no acorns until they reach fifty years of age. What fruits must lie before us!

Stripped from its shell, the turtle that emerged from the sea to lay her eggs in the black sand writhes in the sun, guarded by the boy preparing to tell the story of his first kill.

Who says elephants are the only animals that can't jump?

Pearls melt in vinegar. Women blink twice as much as men. I will always love you.

———————

The shadow of the bridge on which the horse reared up and threw its rider into the abyss is what guides my descendants down through the ages—I who have no name, I who entered history as the begetter of thieves and murderers, I who counted off the animals on the gangplank, I who slept in the common room, I who surveyed the waters draining from the upper slopes of the mountain above which the dove circled, I who wished to call God to account, I who invented hymns for the four winds, I who pitched a tent one night and went off in search of food, I who returned to find blood everywhere, I who am a broken vessel, I who set fire to the withered grass, I who am the scourge of the vineyard and the olive grove, I who fasted for forty days to be granted a vision of nothing, I who know the white heat of the soul and the depths of the cave in which the drawings of the horse, the mammoth, and the bear first appeared, I who saw you there, I who came . . .

Triptych

Not the Horizon

Not the horizon. Only a frayed rope
Hung from the rafters of a burning barn
In which the horses on their hind legs dance
Around a statue of the general
Who led his troops into the stadium
Targeted from a continent away.

Not a museum, not a new beginning,
And not the flare launched by the mariner
Lost off the Outer Banks. Only a clock
In flames on the church wall, telling a story
That we would not repeat to anyone.
Farewell, we told the pilgrims at the door.

Not the subjunctive, not the end, and not
The soldiers standing at attention, scanning
The heavens for a sign. Only an explosion
Muffled by the gears grinding on a barge
Stalled in the locks, sinking with its load of coal.
Not the horizon, not the light, not God.

Not the Light

Not the light, not God—what? Another turning,
Which begins with a pair of apple trees
That didn't make it through the mildest winter
In memory, the branches stiffening
Among the greening lilacs, oaks, and grass:
Kindling with which to start a prairie fire.

Not God, not the conditional, and not
Desire, although desire is integral
To any argument about the divine.
Only a burning hive of bees that hangs
Under the eaves, lighting the cocktail hour
In which a couple signs its living will.

Not illumination. Only fire
Smoldering in the brush beyond the orchard,
Where the mute witnesses of the abuses
Suffered by the devout hide from the scribes,
Who need to draw up lists of the anointed
Before the conflagration can begin.

Not God

Not God, not the imperative, and not
Another trumped-up figure for desire.
Only a ladder propped against the wall
Dividing the holy peninsula
Between the shepherds and the iconographers,
Which the monk climbs upon his tonsuring.

Ancient of Days. The center of the circle.
What the Church Fathers called a radiance
I cannot see this morning through the clouds
Remaining from the storm that swept through town,
Scattering branches and shingles in the street,
And through the grief I feel in this ravine.

Not the divine, not the abyss, and not
The silence ripening in every word.
Only a staircase leading to a door
That overlooks a courtyard choked with weeds
In which love points to the lowering sky.
Not the horizon. Not the light. Not God.

Vacuum

Nature abhors a vacuum; and so what fills this space—dust; lint; cobwebs; calculations; verses from the Psalms; fragments of a theory hatched two centuries ago; the refutation of a heresy no one remembers; sheets of music covered with indecipherable fingerings and erasures; a wooden clock in the shape of a gothic cathedral, carved during the winter in which all the cattle froze to death; a mildewed *kilim* in which opium was smuggled from Anatolia; the last will and testament of the physicist who outlived his heirs; a desk that belonged to a woman who never left her bed—must be ordered and redeemed.

The child who tipped over the ashtray in the tax assessor's office, condemning his parents to penury, came to grief blowing smoke rings through a broken window of a house repossessed by the bank. Nor could he persuade anyone to believe he had gone there to trim the brambles growing over the roof; the lengthy sentence imposed upon him for trespassing he attributed to the judge's criminal ignorance.

How the cellist learned to play so softly that people in the back of the hall would lean forward in their seats to listen, as if to eavesdrop on a conversation between a departing soldier and his wife; how the ushers used their flashlights to pass messages between the councilman and the revolutionary; how the sound engineer who broke their code decided not to betray them to the security agents in the audience; how the recital concluded with a cadenza no one recognized—the signal to the gunmen lurking in the wings.

First they emptied the streets of the capital, arresting every male between the ages of sixteen and sixty, and then they turned the prisons over to interrogators whose linguistic limitations and lack of experience with tribal societies prevented them from identifying the leaders of the insurgency, which was spreading beyond the walls of the city, though they themselves had cut the telephone lines, toppled the radio and television towers, and blocked all the escape routes into the mountains and along the sea.

No sign of the plans drawn up for the occupation, no resolution of the case of the children taken at gunpoint from the school, no chance of the committee issuing its report in time to save anyone. Nor had interest waned in the scandal surrounding the mayor, who went on late-night television to exhibit his collection of vacuum cleaners, which he presented as a history of hygiene and design—a vision of America in line with his theory of progress. He was a true believer. And so we always voted for him.

Buland al-Haydari: *The City Ravaged by Silence*

Baghdad, that captive, forgotten
Between the corpse and the nail.

Baghdad was not besieged by the Persian army
Not seduced by a mare
Nor tempted by a hurricane nor touched by fire.

Baghdad died of a wound from within
From a blind silence that paralyzed the tongues of its children.

That captive was not a homeland
It was just a prison
Wrapped with black walls and guardrails
It was not a night beyond which we say day lies
Baghdad, that captive, forgotten
And ravaged by the silence
Only a desert inhabited by death
Known only to the stones.

One day it almost became . . . at a certain time
A thing in secret
A secret restlessness in the stillness of a room
It almost became a promise in two eyes
A vow in blue films
In which we almost lived a dream
Paper boats borne by the air, flowing
Lightly, seeking no anchor,
No mooring on a bank
We wished it would turn into lightning, revealing desire
But . . .

—Listen . . . listen
And so I listened, and listened closely
But I heard nothing
—Listen . . . listen.

And I laughed . . . Here's the meow of the cat in the neighbor's house
There . . . A rustle of small leaves
Pay no attention . . . It's only the meow of the cat
Only the rustle of the leaves.

A hand knocks on the door four times
The anxious heart pounds a thousand times.

—Listen . . . Don't you hear? Don't you see something . . . ?
I see a shadow lurking behind the window
I can almost see in the dark of its eyes . . . yes
In the darkness of its eyes . . . yes . . . my tear-streaked face
For tomorrow the report will be prepared
The grounds will be prepared for killing you inside us, with us, Oh Baghdad
We must confess, we're the corpse and the nail
And you, forgotten between the corpse and the nail.

—You were awake until the wee hours
—We were awake until the wee hours . . . but we
—What does it mean . . . ? What does it imply . . . ?
On the chair with two broken legs
Above the black table
Near the flickering lantern
There were white papers, yellow papers like pus
There was an open book
Like an exposed secret
And the remains of two pens
What does it mean that you read . . . that you write
That you stay up until dawn
What does it mean . . . ? What does it imply . . . ?

We will be executed in Baghdad's main square
With a signboard larger than Baghdad on both of our chests
(Understand . . . you may not be executed . . . understand . . .
    you may be spared)
You are forbidden to read . . . to write
To talk . . . to cry . . . even to ask
What Baghdad means
What it means to be human or an animal
To be more than a stone forgotten in Baghdad
You are forbidden to be more than the two legs of a harlot
Or the two hands of a pimp.

Baghdad died of a wound inside us . . . of a wound from within
From a blind silence that paralyzed the tongues of its children
Baghdad was ravaged by the silence
So that we have nothing in it, it has nothing in us . . . except death
And the corpse and the nail.

—translated from the Arabic with Hussein Kadhim

All Hallows Eve

Dusk, and a gash of ocher bleeding through
The skin of the white pumpkin left in the patch
Given over to weeds, and husks of corn
Ground into the field harvested last night.
The costumed goblins running up the street
Are not prepared for the first frost. The candle
Burning in the abandoned house casts shadows
Over the cabinets blackened with mildew.
The list of casualties taped to the wall
Outside the recreation center grows.

———————

The myth of innocence was what they cherished—
The noble lie that in their great republic
Nobody tortured prisoners of war,
Or monitored their lawyers' reading lists,
Or eavesdropped on a neighbor's conversation.
Easier to believe in ghosts—in the spirits
Of the original inhabitants
Of a land vouchsafed to them as in a dream
Of their benevolence, an occupation
Approved by all, or so they told themselves.

———————

The maze in which the rat and peacock slept
Through the tornado—rows of corn stalks spared
By an enterprising farmer who discovered
The joy of walking in a labyrinth
On Maui, on his second honeymoon,
In the parking lot of a small wooden church—
Alarms the guardsman's children who have come
On a Sunday school trip to the countryside
So that their mother can prepare the food
For the reception following the wake.

Triptych (2)

Ceremony

At daybreak, when the courtiers demanded
A change of style for every watercourse,
We launched a ship outfitted in the latest
Fashions (flags of convenience sewn with threads
Yanked from the uniforms of our enemies;
Banners proclaiming missions to accomplish
From Babylonia to the Bering Sea;
Sleek long-range missiles tipped with messages
Of condolence for the families sitting down
To dinner in the houses targeted
By an informer who had nursed a grudge
Since the beginning of the revolution),
And as it sailed out of the harbor, toward
The strait in which so many ships had sunk
In the last days of the empire, we ranked
The requests that we would forward to the new
Authorities: roses and a sack of wine
For the translator who had confused the terms
Of the peace treaty that could not be signed;
A cabin by the sea for the fabulist
Who thought we would be welcomed everywhere
As the architects of an enduring order;
And sheaves of handmade paper for the scribes
Who might have led us to the next frontier,
If only they had found their pens in time.

On the Military Commissions Act of 2006

The brown recluse trapped in the reading room
Of the library, where a lecturer
On human rights was searching for the names

Of three ghost prisoners interrogated
Somewhere in Central Asia and forgotten,
Returned to the locked cabinet, the wall
Of glass and wood beyond which lay a haven
Where it could winter among manuscripts
And codices collected from the tower
Of a monastery razed in the Middle Ages;
And when it could not clear the wall, it spun
About, pivoting on an axis of dust
Until its six eyes focused on the chair
In which the lecturer, imagining
That his research would preserve the memory
Of what was once espoused in our name, stretched
His legs and gazed at the late autumn light
Streaming through the high windows, and the motes
Suspended in the air, and the hooded shadows
Cast on the volumes open on the table.

Mortar

Launched from the ruins of an insane asylum,
Above a city under the command
Of a proconsul who did not have time
To learn the local language or the customs,
The mortar arcs toward the marketplace,
Where the old women hunch over their stalls,
Arranging their displays of vegetables
And fruits that arrived from the countryside
On horse-drawn carts, under cover of darkness;
Of beef and cognac smuggled in by soldiers
Who would rather trade with their former neighbors
Than shoot more gravestones in the cemetery;
Of olive oil collected from a ravaged
Village, where human rights investigators
Are taking testimony from survivors,
Gathering evidence for a tribunal

Which is already running short on funds;
Of sacks of humanitarian supplies
Spirited out of an unguarded warehouse;
Of doilies sewn by refugees, and puppets
Assembled by candlelight in borrowed flats,
And military souvenirs from the last
Order—the medals and insignia
Coveted by the man who fired the mortar.

Logbook

A wooden sailboat riding low in the water, between the harbor and the barrier island given over to great blue herons and wild horses. Someone made off with the logbook, in which a history was recorded in the invisible ink of desire: the scandal surrounding the maiden voyage from London; the ports of call in which the fleeing family took refuge; their decision to dry-dock in Casablanca for the duration of the war they did not survive; the new owner's murky references; how he outfitted the boat to deliver armed insurgents to Albania; how it was stripped of the contraband he picked up off the coast of Peru; the foolishness of the authorities in St. Kitt's who allowed him to escape; the changes in the weather on the night his boat capsized near Fiji and he disappeared; the discoveries of the marine biologist who sailed to Savannah, where the boat was torched by a slave trader's descendant, then tugged north by a salvage company along the Intercoastal Waterway . . . The *George III* is peeling black paint from its bow to its stern and boards from all of its portholes. No one knows why it was named after the king. And who can explain why the tide is redder than the morning sky? Sand drifts into the channel; the sprawl dredged from the point covers the dying trees and marsh grass in which the horses search for water. The sea is rising, rising. A heron glides over the oyster flats. The war will never end.

II

In Memory of Donald Justice

A stitch in time may save a rhyme
From the graver faults of pantomime—

Exaggerated facial tics
And nods: the stuff of politics.

For what unravels in a verse,
Like crepe de chine left in a hearse,

Is not what can embroider thought
And feeling but what can't be taught:

That music is intrinsic to
The very way we say I do,

And then do not until it is
Too late to change direction—viz,

Love, marriage, war. That we betray
Ourselves and others is no stay

Against confusion or remorse
But fit for study in a course

Devoted to the poetry
Of the sublime, a deity

That has inspired no shortage of
Bad poems on the theme of love.

Though not by you. For you could tell
A broken clapper from a bell.

And you revealed at every turn
Of phrase and folly how we burn

To know the meaning of that line—
A stitch in time saves nine.

Three Questions

And if there is no change in our condition?

Seven hang-gliders set their sights on a lodge
Boarded up since the war, twisting and floating
On an updraft that swirls them past a cliff
From which a forest ranger monitors
Lightning strikes, smoke, and wind: the stealthy progress
Of a fire spreading from a mountaintop
To a ravine and then along the dry
Fork of a river over which the gliders
May soon sail in formation, casting shadows
Dark as the clouds building on the horizon.

And if we cannot find an antidote?

The private amphitheater was full,
Although nobody knew who would perform,
Or why they had received an invitation,
In an elaborate script, to donate their time,
Not money, to a cause they had not heard of—
The restoration of a style of thought
Discovered in the War Between the States,
Secreted in a hand-sewn packet of letters
Addressed to God, and then bequeathed to those
Willing to forge, *at the White Heat,* a soul.

And if our final words are not recorded?

The traveler had stowed his overcoat,
Cane, and valise behind a wooden cage
(In which two sparrows, fluttering their wings
Whenever the train whistle sounded, sang
Until the other passenger in the compartment

Draped over them a curtain of black crepe),
And drifted into sleep, dreaming of silos,
And icebergs calving in Antarctica,
And pages burning in the Book of the Dead,
Including the page on which his name was entered.

Valves

for David Skorton

Valves of the heart, which regulate the flow of blood from the distant reaches of the body, with the pulsing of a star whose light travels toward us long after it has gone out; of the alpenhorn, French horn, trumpet, clarinet, saxophone, and bassoon, raising and lowering pitches as precisely as the bridgetender at the controls, watching for the approach of the schooner bulging with spices, sugar, and rum from the New World; of the steam plant, governing the pressure that powers the city by the river so that men and women, rising from sleep, can switch on the lights and start their day. Like eyes, they open and close; like mouths, they are always working.

How the sea circulating through the oysters in the estuary is filtered and cleansed; how the shells pile up, like books, along the tidal flat to be picked over by egrets and great blue herons; how the inlet surges and ebbs, subject to the wind, whims of the moon, and the freighter's wake; how the port links its history of piracy and slave trading to the fishing boats and ships carrying marine biologists and their students to the Gulf Stream: another valve in a system of valves.

If the poet purifies the dialect of the tribe, then poetry is a valve through which words regain their luster. Likewise the lines of the painter opening new perspectives on the mountain rising beyond the fortifications of rock and tree; the grace notes of the composer who heard blossoms falling at the departure of the beloved; the arabesques of the dancer who fled the war zone; the monologue delivered by an actor in an empty theater; the spinning of the blind potter's wheel; the sinuous gestures of the shadow puppeteer certain to be imprisoned.

Equations and formulas, prescriptions and recipes, rites and rituals: these roll off the tongues of the scholars, scientists, and clerics charged with administering our inheritance. Bless them. And bless the evaluators, inventors, reformers, scribes, prophets, and zealots, with their forms, patents, writs, reams of paper, spells, and incantations, with which they bring order to the universe. And channels, bridges, canals, sluices, tubes, accelerators, stoppers, plugs: the whole apparatus of locks and passages in which cargo is transported, crowds assemble and disperse, waters rise and fall, experiments are conducted, atoms whirl, liquids turn into gas.

A valve opens in the earth, and lava flows into the sea to create an island, home to spores and seeds borne on the wind from a thousand miles away. The double doors are never closed in the provinces ruled by the god of fire, where barberries line the slopes of a volcano swelling with ash, which will erupt and rise in a plume toward the meteor entering the atmosphere with a payload of elements with which to start anew. Flue and funnel, throat and threshold: What enters? What remains? A history of windows and walls. An essay on the gates—of lovemaking, of birth, of death—through which we pass. Does this not instruct? Delight?

Diptych

Poem Beginning with a Line by My Daughter, Abigail

When I wake up, I'm still asleep.
And when I get dressed, my clothes are missing.
And when I finish breakfast, I'm always hungry.
And when I walk to school, the street is empty.
And when I open my book, the pages are blank.
And when I count the boys in my class, the walls are blue.
And when I count the girls in my class, the walls are yellow.
And when the bell rings for recess, the playground is gone.
And when I come home, the house is dark.
And when I open the mail, the lights switch on.
And when I try to whistle, my mouth becomes a balloon.
And when I begin to sing, the balloon sails out the window.
And when I enter the garden, the flowers turn their backs on me.
And when I pet my cat, she flaps her wings and flies away.
And when I call my dog, a wolf lopes out of the woods.
And when I sit down to dinner, the table is crowded with people I don't know.
And when I ask for dessert, everybody claps their hands.
And when I climb into bed, I'm wide awake.

Poem Ending with a Line by President George W. Bush

The screening of the film on genocide,
Designed to build momentum for the final
Lecture at the festival of human rights,
Was marred by the projectionist's refusal
To dim the lights in the auditorium.
We looked around, confused, until someone quoted
The president: *There's no cave deep enough*
For America, or dark enough to hide.

Proclamation

Whereas a pair of biplanes flying side by side on a summer morning, one yellow, one red, their wings nearly touching as the pilots banked wide turns in tandem, inspired a man on a bridge to gaze into the blue sky;

Whereas he was experiencing a crisis of faith, not with the tenets enunciated in the Gospels but with the church affiliation he had inherited from his mother, along with her pride, myopia, and fear of heights;

Whereas he was a scribe given to praising the qualities of mint and anise and cumin instead of seeking justice, mercy, and faith, preferring to savor the aromas in his kitchen to the possibility of discovering an enduring structure of meaning;

Whereas once in a foreign capital he walked through the rubble of a library razed in a civil war, never imagining that such destruction would be visited upon his own house;

Whereas he passed up a chance on a pilgrimage to restore a Byzantine mosaic of the Harrowing of Hell, choosing to climb a mountain he had climbed before, not to glimpse a doorway into eternity but for the sake of exercising his body;

Whereas his family expected to trace the letters of his name chiseled on a wall memorializing the victims of a conflict no one understood;

Whereas he could not tell if the angry crowd approaching the bridge was heading for the cathedral or the stadium into which the homeless had been herded;

Whereas the pilots flew on to view *the latest scenes of devastation*, circling above a fleet of wooden ships sailing down a highway flooded by the surging river, their biplanes buffeted by winds left over from the storm;

Whereas their wings brushed against each other, lightly, lightly;

Whereas this kiss and caress, this marriage of spars and ribs, sent them spiraling earthward, toward a sheet of water spreading from the city to the plains;

Whereas new life forms were evolving in this inland sea, feeding on the solvents that poured out of a plant engulfed in water and flames—enigmas thrashing in the rainbow-colored pools of oil in which the future was designing its flags;

Whereas the committee charged with determining what was detrimental to the public good ignored the work of the scribe on the bridge, who hid between the railings until the men with baseball bats had crossed to the other side;

Whereas he recorded in his notebook the number of charred timbers, chairs, and files floating past, among the water moccasins and empty rowboats;

Whereas he took refuge in a white tent pitched by soldiers recalled from the war;

Whereas he recited certain words from the liturgy—*The doors, the doors*—until they moved into his heart and began to govern his breathing;

Therefore let us pray for him, and for the pilots and sailors, the refugees and marauders, the living and the dead, now and in the Age to Come.

Three Nonsense Poems

for Hannah and Abigail

How much mush is too much mush
If you love mush too much?
How much slush is too much slush
If you love slush and such?
Hush, my child, don't rush to brush
Your mush into the slush. That's too much!

———————

Now I will take my ease,
Out in the garden, please,
Among the birds and bees,
Which only want to tease,
Making up rhymes like these:
Tall as the Pyrenees,
Small as a Pekingese,
Wide as antipodes,
Thin as a zebra's knees,
Bright as a set of keys,
And with such rhymes as these,
Why I . . . Why I . . . I sneeze!

———————

It's dark in the park,
And the cat is fat—
Bees in the trees
And a rat in the vat.
The cow will meow
At the horse on the course.
But the pig with the fig

And the bat in the hat
Will roll through the hole
Deep into sleep.

Report

A fisherman baited his hook from the sandbar in the middle of the river, while the freight train stalled on the trestle above him rocked back and forth, its wheels squealing under the livestock on their way to the slaughterhouse.

Swallows skimmed along the foaming water by the power plant, preparing a new report on the state of the earth.

The drought was in its third month, the fields had turned brown, the river was drying up; steam rose from the tundra, glaciers receded, and icebergs melted in the warming seas, in which bells tolled for the sharks and sturgeon, rays and drums.

Meanwhile the prisoners, who had used tent poles to dig a tunnel, hauling dirt up in water jugs to spread on the soccer field, were caught just before they attempted to escape.

So they fashioned slingshots out of strips of canvas, loaded socks with dirt and feces, tore up floorboards to use as shields, and waited for the signal to begin.

The uprising lasted for three days until a helicopter ferrying troops from the desert swept into the courtyard, its rotor flattening the tents in which the prisoners took aim at the guards, hurling stones, chunks of cinderblock, and burning socks.

I will ask you one thing, Jesus said to the chief priests and scribes, *which if you tell Me, I likewise will tell you by what authority I do these things.*

For He had brought the blind and the lame into the temple, which they were not allowed to enter, and healed them, infuriating the authorities.

Who could not answer His question, widening the abyss between them.

And because for some the issue of His legitimacy would never be resolved the question still hangs in the air, like the swirling motes the child first noticed in the shaft of sunlight brightening his bedroom as he was leaving for school.

Hence the limbs falling from the dying oak may be used to bank a fire, refute a heresy, or attack the scientific method—if not to build a bridge from this world to the next.

And hence the great blue heron taking flight toward the driftwood piled on the riverbank inscribes in the air this command: *Obey, obey.*

Three Horses

I am the mare night forgot—blessed
Brooding, brilliant. Remembered.

I am the colt women corral, leaving
Paradise, believing everything.

I am the last steed Athena mounted
—Galloper, ascending, enraptured.

Diptych (2)

Lines for Jane and Jonathan Wells

How the white horses gallop through the city
At nightfall, when the fog rolls in from the sea
And one by one the street lamps fail to light.

The curtain of the port rises on nothing—
No buoys and no boats. Only the cry
Of a gull flying somewhere over the water,

And then the whinnying of the last horse
Rearing before the gate it will pass through
On its hind legs to join the rest of the herd.

Only this—and the light above your door.

Lines on the Death of Ingmar Bergman

A woman sketching, a man steeped in gin—
Note how the final scene assembling
In the rain shadow of a mountain range
Ablaze from ridge to ridge carries no hint
Of the catastrophe: the smoke, the wind.

Nor do the daily rushes, catalogued
For a committee of historians
Attempting to discern the exact moment
Of the republic's death, contain instructions
For the executor of the estate—

The editor, that is, who was unwisely
Sacked on the second day of shooting, then hired
By the filmmaker's estranged wife to save
From the approaching fire a commentary
On eschatology: *The Seventh Seal.*

Notes for a Lecture on Eschatology

Inertia

No anchorage along this coast, and no
Desire to sail home or around the cape
At night. No rope with which to scale the cliff
Or hang the prisoner locked in the hold,
Between the vats of salted meat and water,
Who only dreamed of crossing the Red Sea.
No instructions for the diplomats
Examining the maps spread on their bunks.
No orders for the cabin boy and chef.
No plans to celebrate the elevation
Of the cross stored in pieces below deck.
And no way now to find the pond in the grove
Of eucalyptuses, where the lovers made
A shrine out of their clothes before they swam
To the waterfall and, embracing in the spray,
Conceived a plan destined to drive them apart,
Then dried each other with a strip of bark.
Nothing to do. Nowhere to go. No one.

Four o'Clock

The thief was loping toward the crowded square,
Past open-air cafés and restaurants
In which economists and civil servants
From the Ministry of Information were joking
With poets and professors of translation,
When the watchmaker trailing him cried out—
To no avail. The patrons looked around,
Perplexed, wondering what was true. No one
Doubted the thief would get away with it.
They checked their watches. It was getting late.

Lines on a Friend's Retirement

for Bill Decker

Now that the work is done—the papers filed,
The garden harvested, the tools returned
To the garage—and the formalities
Complete (the clearing out, the taking leave),
The grand entanglements of love and loss
Obscured by the routines of any calling
Will weave new threads for you, not to protect
The heart (which may be worn now on the sleeve)
But to reveal the pattern and design
Of a deliberate walk in the sun
And all the landmarks glimpsed along the way—
Mist rising from the thawing river, a great
Blue heron gliding toward the railroad trestle,
The fisherman baiting his hook again . . .

Intermission

Take off your clothes, the magician told the crowd
In the unheated auditorium,
While his assistant dripped hot wax on the stage.
The lights were dimmed. The ushers swept down the aisles,
Collecting business suits and evening dresses,
Underwear, jewelry, shoes. The goatherd's daughter
Leaned over the balcony to throw a vase
Into the pit, where the musicians hired
At the last minute waited for the conductor
To return from the negotiating table.
The assistant waved a candle like a baton.
The customs officer sat on his hands.
The set designer counted up the coffins
Stacked in the wings, among the mannequins.
Wisdom. Attend, repeated the magician.

The Ideal Reader

for Nataša Ďurovičová and Garrett Stewart

The rigging was incomprehensible
To the deckhand hired in the Windward Islands,
And so the schooner drifted into the sea lane
In which a warship from the imperium
Was firing on the empty garrison
Above the walled city. The councilors
Locked themselves in the tower. Men and women
Gathered their children and a few belongings
And hurried to the gate. Shells whistled overhead.
The deckhand tugged a rope to no avail,
While a woman closed the window in her kiosk,
Opened her new book, and began to read.

The Ruins

All's aslant—the tilted shade of the lamp
Flickering in the living room; the flashing
Torn from the chimney and the roof; the rain
That lodges in the walls. How far I've strayed
From everything I loved. The ceiling sags
Under boxes of correspondence. Leaves
Fall on the stalks of the sunflowers severed
In the wind storm. The turret of a tank
Parked on the ruins of a theater
Swivels to aim at the archaeologists
Entering stage left, where the prophet waved
A rod cut from an almond tree. Called
To root out and pull down, to build and plant,
He would become a city unto himself,
Walled off from everyone. A car packed with explosives
Stalls at a school. A teacher squints. Nothing.

The Boats

The courtyard sloped away from God. And the sea
Was black with boats slipped from their moorings. An icon
Sailed upright from Byzantium, bearing
The good news of a woman bound in chains
Who vowed to free the muralists condemned
At the feast celebrating their commission
To paint the churches whitewashed in the last
Campaign on terror. And though the scribe had no time
To reflect on his role in the uprising
Before the legionnaires imprisoned him,
From his cell above the courtyard he could watch
The boats drift into port, clogging the sea-lanes,
And think what little difference it made
That he had loved that woman for so long.
The coffin-makers worked all night. A priest
Arrived to hear the muralists' confessions.
The woman climbed the chains inside the tower
To call out to the executioner
—In vain. The cisterns cracked. The living water
Flowed away. The boats sailed out of sight.

Variation on a Theme by Vallejo and Justice

Christopher Merrill will die one afternoon
Not in his sleep, as he had hoped, and not
With someone reading the Psalms over him,
But in a holdup at a bank machine,
Or when his car skids off an icy road,
Or as he shuts the door to the garage
And calls the ancient family dog to heel.

Christopher Merrill is dead. He died last night,
Last week, last year—the date remains uncertain.
Nor did the earth receive him as a guest
But as an interloper who had learned
To hide his true intentions from his friends
And family. And now he is a story
No one tells. Christopher Merrill is dead.

He had a heart attack, a burst appendix,
A fall from a high ledge into a canyon
In which a flash flood swept his body away,
Secreting it in a cave, in a pile of rubbish
Under a wall of petroglyphs of charred horses,
And bears, and the flute player who traded feathers
For seeds. No one will ever find it.

Paul Celan: *Eight Romanian Prose Poems*

I

Raphael came by the night before the deportations were supposed to begin, dressed in a vast desolation of black silk, with a hood. His fiery gazes crisscrossed my forehead, wine streamed down my cheeks, spread over the ground, people sipped it in their sleep. —Come, said Raphael, draping over my blinding shoulders a desolation like his. I bent toward my mother, kissed her incestuously, and fled. A swarm of big black tropical butterflies slowed my steps. Raphael dragged me after him, and we descended to the railway. I felt the tracks underfoot, I heard the whistle of a locomotive closing in, my heart froze. The train passed overhead.

I opened my eyes. Before me, on a wide plain, was a giant candelabrum with thousands of branches. —Is it gold? I whispered to Raphael. —Gold. Climb one branch so that when I have raised it in the air you can hook it to the sky. Before daybreak, people will save themselves by flying there. I'll show them the way, and you'll receive them.

I climbed a branch, Raphael went from one branch to the next, touching them in turn, the candelabrum began to rise. A leaf fell on my forehead, just where my friend's gaze had touched me, a maple leaf. I look around: this can't be the sky. Hours pass, and I've found nothing. I know: people are gathering down there, Raphael touched them with his thin fingers, they also ascended, but I haven't stopped yet.

Where is the sky? Where?

II

Without a banister, the immense stairs—on which the ethereal flag of your encounter with yourself rises and falls—are the only certain coordinates of the movements still tempting me. Yet I accept them without a banister, I even prefer them for my rare strolls between Cancer and Capricorn, when at odds with the season I flood the house with the black lace of the pleasure of loving no one. Equally rare, but under an inner sky marked by a magical wand, I descend, a burning wheel, to the extreme edge of the steps, the very bottom, where the hair of the woman I killed waits to strangle me. I avoid the danger with a cunning that my heirs will not inherit. Then I climb back to the top step and repeat the performance at greater and greater speeds until I make a spectacular mockery of the locks on the last step. Now—and only now—am I visible to those who, hating me for a long time, eagerly await the finale. But unaccustomed to this sort of event, they believe I'm the metal banister and, oblivious to the danger, they descend to the very bottom and fling open the door through which the Illustrious Dead will enter.

III

Maybe one day, when the rehabilitation of solstices becomes official, dictated by the ferocity with which people fight the trees of the grand blue boulevards, maybe then all four of you will commit suicide at the same time, tattooing the hour of death on the leafy skin of your foreheads, like Spanish dancers, tattooing the hour with the arrows—still timid, but no less poisonous—of the adolescence of a goodbye . . .

Maybe I'll be around, maybe you'll already have announced the great event so I can be there when your eyes, buried in the remote rooms of the greenhouse in which, throughout your life, you freely exiled yourselves to contemplate the eternal immobility of northern palms, tell the world about the imperishable beauty of the somnambulant tigers . . . Maybe I'll find the courage to contradict you then, at the moment when, after so many fruitless expectations, we find a common language. It's up to you if I spread my fingers like a fan and stir the faintly salted breeze of the requiem for the victims of the first rehearsal of the end. And it's also up to you if I drop my handkerchief into your mouths, devastated by the fire of false prophesies, and, later, out in the street, wave it over the coalescing heads of the crowd, when they gather around the town's only fountain to look, one by one, at the last drop of water on the bottom. I'll wave it always in silence, with gestures banishing any other message.

It's up to you. Believe me.

IV

Once again I hang the big white umbrellas in the night air. I know, Columbus's new route doesn't lead this way, my archipelago will remain undiscovered. The endless ramifications of the aerial roots, from which I hang by one hand then the other, will embrace in solitude, unknown to the seekers of the heights, the hands will clutch more and more convulsively and will never again give up their gloves of melancholy. I know this, just as I know I can't trust the tides that, with foam churned up from the bottom, bathe the lacy shores of these islands which should belong to authoritarian sleep. Under my bare feet the sand begins to burn. I rise up on my toes and drift over there. I can't expect hospitality, I know that, too, but where should I stop if not over there? They don't receive me. An unknown messenger waits at sea to tell me every port is forbidden to me. I offer him my hands bleeding from the floating thorns of the nocturnal sky in exchange for a moment of rest, hoping that from the silky shore of my first parting from myself I can hoist up a row of billowing sails and continue my journey. I offer my hands to see that the equilibrium of this posthumous flora is preserved from danger. Once again I'm rejected. I have no choice but to keep traveling, but my strength is exhausted, and I close my eyes to look for a man with a boat.

V

You might think that everything said about the tree of heaven would be enough to cancel your vacation. You emptied the sources of light from the mirror, you loved singing the acrostic of the sinless traveler in the fragrances, sad and clear-eyed as the onion flower, you sighed on the occasion of the kerchiefs fluttering in the gardens, you called Mariana, you called her with a color spread out with the ink of life, but you forgot that a room is not a tree, that you eat its foliage with the spoon of memory, that the doors facing south have no keys. You could have stepped over their threshold before the dawns were overwhelmed by embalmed soarings, you could have poured yourself out at the same time as the lakes in the walls, could have jumped with the snowballs lost in the eyes of the man-eating bushes, could have said once more—for the last time—the word hanging from the transparent icon of your restless neck: "rust." But rusty was the desert where you wandered, your sandal contaminated by the poetry of a paper adolescence, rusty was the adolescent paper from which you stepped up to the threshold. So you gave up.

You decided to climb the tree without taking the risks of a stargazer. The stars . . . How often you wanted to remember their flashing eclipse in the honey laid over the poisonious table . . . It was one of the things that made you abandon the city—in daylight, in the plain sight of everyone, with your suitcase crammed into your brain, your pencil hovering over the amalgam of wax and the first quarter of the moon.

How cheery it was to scatter the glasses with a murmur on the hexagonal tombstone of love. No one saw you. You wandered alone through the streets guarded by enormous umbrellas, the parachutes of the dwarfs descended again to the earth. There was a rumor in the air, a rumor of bachelor coins coming to see you leave. You stopped for a moment to gaze at them: your jacket was unbuttoned—how else could you satisfy the lacy curiosity of your chest? They told you about black birds and fox holes. Stubborn and infatuated by the allogenic extremities of strolling, you thought the moment had come to find them, despite the paralyzing legacies. Wrong again.

Didn't you notice your steps advancing on downy boredom? That the vast room of possibilities, jeopardized by hawks with earrings, no longer suited the flag thrust into the pond with people disguised as motor boats? Didn't you understand that as a traveler you were subject to the leprous curtain of blood-stained tents? Ah, no one was in the tent? Was the rival's raven on the heraldry at the entrance? With hair the color of tea turned yellow in the light of the birdless hour? Was an act of monosyllabic courage required? A tour of the plundered landscape of impulses near the poppy? Yes, it's hard to find a place where sand pampered in coal hands is preserved. It's hard to carry the orphaned dreams of mourning eye sockets. It's hard . . .

But tell me, you who knew how to wave your polished atrocities and glitter, you, obsessed by intervals of time brimming with the small-toothed fish of leafless news, you, messenger of abscesses blooming with the salt of tears—answer:

Who drowned first? Who went down the steps with disheveled

hair and hardened posterity's undulations? Who fled from the beloved on a horse stolen from the neighbors? Who snuck around the mantel, and . . . *(The text ends here; the next page is missing.)*

VI

At last, the moment has come—before the mirrors covering the outside walls of the house in which you left your beloved, disheveled forever—to hoist your dark flag from the top of the early blooming acacia. You can hear, sharply, the fanfare of the blind regiment, the only one that remained faithful to you, you put on your mask, fasten the black lace to the sleeves of your suit of ash, climb the tree, the flag enfolds you, the flight begins. No, no one ever knew how to flutter around this house like you. Night falls, you float on your back, the mirrors of the house lean over to pick up your shadow, shooting stars tear your mask, your eyes drain into your heart where the sycamore set fire to its leaves, stars are falling there, too, every one of them until the last, a smaller bird, death, gravitates around you, and your dreamy mouth pronounces your name.

VII

Partisan of erotic absolutism, megalomaniac reticent even among the divers, messenger of Paul Celan's halo, I evoke the petrifying physiognomies of the aerial shipwreck only once a decade (or more), and I only skate at a very late hour, on a lake watched over by the giant forest of the acephalous members of the Universal Poetic Conspiracy. It's easy to understand why you can't penetrate there with arrows of a visible fire. An immense amethyst curtain conceals, at the edge of the world, the existence of this anthropomorphic vegetation, beyond which I attempt to perform, selenographically, a dance to amaze me. I haven't succeeded yet and, with my eyes set back in my temples, I gaze at myself in profile, waiting for spring.

—March 11, 1947

VIII

There were nights when it seemed to me your eyes, under which I drew large dark orange bags, were about to ignite their ashes again. Those nights there was less rain. I would open the windows and climb, naked, onto the window sill to look out at the world. The trees of the forest would march toward me, one by one, obedient, a defeated army come to lay down its arms. I stayed still, and the sky lowered its flag under which the armies fought. From one corner you watched me, too, as I stood there, beautifully bleeding in the nude: I was the only constellation extinguished by the rain, I was the Southern Cross. But those nights it was hard to open your veins when the flames covered me, the citadel of urns was mine, I filled it with my blood after dismissing the enemy army, rewarding it with cities and harbors, the silver panther tore up the dawns lying in wait for me. I was Petronius, and I was shedding my blood again among the roses. For each stained petal you extinguished a torch.

Do you remember? I was Petronius, and I didn't love you.

—translated from the Romanian with Magda Cârneci

Notes for an Essay on Faith

Lines for Eddin Khoo

How we believe, and what, and why: a sacred
Triad by which to organize a life,
A world—the garland strung with saffron, rose,
And jasmine hanging from the statue of Kali;
The rooster scratching at the post; the baby
Calling the priestess from her ministrations
Toward the goddess: the lighting of the lamps;
The ringing of the bell; and the honoring,
At dusk, of the king cobra slithering
Out of the gutter to worship in this temple . . .

Lines for Isaac the Blind

The letters of the Hebrew alphabet
Inspired the fingerings a violinist
Inscribed—in secret—in a soldier's score
Before he was deployed to a desert cave
To fast for forty days, sustained by prayer:
An arch extending from this world to the next.
And the letters are like branches, said the blind
Kabbalist. And the tree is growing still
In the silence deepening after the final chord.

Sale Day

The auctioneer had lost his voice. And the lambs
Balked at the distance to the holding pen.
Prices were falling faster than the sky.
The old man marked his card, then folded it

Into a square to be deposited
In the collection plate on Sunday morning.
The lot is cast into the lap, he groaned
When a pair of goats was led around the pen
To coax the lambs inside. The auctioneer
Cleared his throat. A buyer raised his hand.
The old man stood, shaking his head. *The whole
Disposing thereof is of the Lord,* he said.

Cross

This dried palm frond twisted into a T;
This cross bleached by the sun through the oak leaves
And sidelong slats of the Venetian blinds;
This sign and herald of another order
Arranged among four sand dollars on a desk
Bought at a church auction—it bears the good
News of the sea: two young men in the surf
At dusk, rocking a sailboat off a sandbar,
While a woman on a white mare gallops past,
Determined to forget the rioting
And the wrath called down by the man of God
Chastising unbelievers in the square.

Icon

Locked in the treasury, the handless saint
Reads from a scroll the names of those he must
Learn to forgive: the novice who pocketed
The key to the refectory; the caliph
Whose torturer could not obey an order;
The architect of the inheritance
Laws that delivered him to poverty.
There is no way to trim the candlewick.

And who will heed his cry above the chanting
Of the monks burning in the tower? *Priests*
Of the invisible, hear this prayer . . .

Lines on the Death of Pope John Paul II

A flash of red—a cardinal in the catkins!
The branches of the white oak, like an inverted
Chalice, pour the warm contents of the air
Over the street, where the peeling macadam
Reveals the brickwork of the first believers
In this community. The birthday party
Next door is in full swing. A chickadee
Bobs on a yellow spray, then flies beyond
The magnolia opening to the sky.
Asleep against the fence, the old dog whimpers
As a mole churns through the softening earth
Beneath her belly. The noon siren blares.

Lines along the Way

Three crosses on a hill below a field
Of corn ready for harvesting. And bales
Of hay arranged likes books beyond the fence
Draped with the carcass of a wolverine.
And sumac reddening, like a bandage. A ribbon
Of white dust rises from the county road
Behind a pickup driving home from church.
Goats and cattle graze around the tower
Built for the Early Warning System. *Eternity,*
The billboard reads, *is a long time to be wrong.*

Advent Stanzas

Ringlets of ice, like water lily pads,
Drift down the freezing Susquehanna. Wax
Drips from the candles in the packed cathedral,
Burning the children's hands. The retired banker
Dozes on the sofa, while his neighbor hacks
Into his computer to read his tax return.
False balances are an abomination
Before the Lord, a woman chants, hanging
The stockings from the flintlock on the mantel,
But a just weight is acceptable unto him.

———————

What's God's phone number? asked the sleepless child.
One, one, one, said her father. So she dialed
The other world, discovering the routing
Is always through this world. *Today,* she sang,
Replacing the receiver, *is tomorrow.*
Her father smiled, examining the row
Of numbers foretelling his demise. A bell
Rang by the river. His daughter took his hand.
A star shall come forth out of Jacob, and
A scepter shall rise out of Israel . . .

———————

They waited in the desert for a sign
To guide them through the winter night. Alone
In the universe, or so they feared, the nomads
Scanning the constellations for the seeds
Of new life destined to take root and grow
In their dry souls, blossoming here below
Like flowers that appear after a fire,

Pointed to one red star, and then another,
And then—and then they cried out to the stones:
For He will save his people from their sins . . .

Nativity Stanzas

Pieces of insulation cling to the tree,
Like honeycombs—debris from the tornado
That flattened the garage before it skipped
Across the river and tore up the hill
Below the renovated capitol,
Heralding the birth of a new order
In which the differences between each side
In a debate on spiritual matters
Would be exaggerated for the sake
Of seeing someone fall upon his sword.

———

The legislators moved their desks again
Moments before the rebels fired a mortar,
Which pierced the roof and struck the podium
On which the general's medals were displayed—
For courage under fire, for a decision
To settle a dispute without resorting
To war, for faith in the enduring wisdom
Of Scripture—beside the founding documents
Of a republic destined to create
Havoc in every corner of the earth.

———

The boy constructing a treehouse lay down
His hammer and handsaw on the first day
Of summer to drink from the outside faucet
A gust of air, bees, bits of honeycomb,
And then the rusted water sputtering
Into his mouth to douse the fire and rinse
The old words forming on his swelling tongue—

Words like *God, damn, hell, Jesus Christ,* and *Mary,*
Which he could use to divide or unite,
And which might summon him to another life.

Lenten Stanzas

A rivulet of snow in a scorched hillside;
A hawk alighting on a traffic sign;
The ice unlocking in the reservoir—
Open, open! A day and a day. And rain
Dousing the prairie fires, smoke shrouding the road.
To pray without distraction is my prayer:
Kyrie, eleison. Kyrie, eleison. Kyrie, eleison . . .

———————

The snakes slithered out of the copper mine
To strike the tribesmen fleeing from God's wrath—
Locusts, Egyptian bondsmen, scorpions.
Thus the prophet raised a statue, a bronze
Serpent, the sight of which could heal the stricken.
From death to life eternal: a new path—
For God so loved the world that he gave his only Son . . .

———————

From the top floor of the Ministry of Trade
A sniper fires into the silent crowd;
An arsonist compares notes with a looter;
A scribe plans to betray a chorister—
In this interpretation of the law
Only the martyr can remember the Way.
Father, forgive them, for they know not what they do . . .

Stanzas in Penitence

The empty vase in the window of the house
Propped on the flatbed driving down the street
Picks up the voices in the telephone wires
Clipped by the gable roof: *Where are you, love?*
No, not today. Yes, an emergency!
The foreman walks under the moving house
Muttering, *That which the cankerworm hath left . . .*

———————

The violinist on the frozen lake
Rehearses in white gloves a requiem
For the lost children and the unbegotten,
While fish are hauled up in a net and loaded
Onto a dogsled pulled by old men taken
Prisoner in a war no one remembers,
Who sing: *And I will restore to you the years . . .*

———————

Hey, you! the cop cries, jabbing his night stick
Into the corpse afloat at the river's edge.
The crowd shivering by the iron railing
Taunts the ballooning clothes, the nape of the neck.
Wake up, the cop calls. *You can't sleep here.* The corpse
Bobs in the water. Ice floes sail to the sea.
Why do you think evil in your hearts?

Lines on Cheese-Fare Saturday

A peregrine falcon perched on a sign
Along the highway—*God is Pro-Life: Are You?*—
Scans the field burned last week for the spring planting.
A freight train carrying coal across the prairie
Wobbles in the wind, and black dust coats the flag
Raised on the sandbar of the thawing river.
The armor plating factory is hiring.

———————

When he had given everything away
And settled in a cave far from the city,
Among the snakes and scorpions escaping
The desert heat, he undertook the work
Of virtue—fasting, praising God, and weaving
Baskets out of palm fronds gathered at the oasis,
Where the servant girls and soldiers met each night.

———————

Let us praise the assemblies of holy fathers—
God-bearing men whose lives of prayer, discernment,
And illumination may help us to attend
To the first green shoots pushing through the litter
Of leaves and snowmelt on the path through the woods:
Anthony, Euthymius, and all the saints
Who teach the art of fasting and repentance.

Maundy Thursday

The tornado touched down at nightfall, on the west bank of the river, and blazed a trail through the city.

And as it shattered windows; ripped roofs from houses and trees from roots; upended cars and buses; toppled the clock tower; swirled around a park, splintering a gazebo in which a family had taken shelter—a priest led his parishioners to the basement of his church.

And as the winds flattened a gas station, a taco stand, a dance studio; hurled rafters through a cement wall; lifted the pipe organ from another church, set it down in the street, and continued eastward—the priest washed the feet of the faithful, celebrating the Messiah's love of His disciples.

They sang hymns in the dark, maintaining their vigil until dawn.

An irruption into history, a breaking into a before and an after, a moment unto itself.

Which they would attempt to describe to themselves and to one another until they settled on a storyline agreeable to all—

How the myth by which they lived must be revised: that the city would be spared because of its river and hills, its architecture and guilds, its markets brimming with the bounty of harvests from every land . . .

They were afraid for . . . The original version of the Gospel breaks off in the middle of the sentence; no translation conveys the terror of the women emerging from the empty tomb to a world lit by a new dispensation, the meaning of which lay in the future, if at all.

Perhaps on a Maundy Thursday, in the new millennium, when a funnel cloud appeared on the horizon of a city whose inhabitants had ceased to believe that natural disasters might befall them.

Thus they lacked provisions: batteries, enough dry goods and bottled water to last a week, bandages for the cuts they suffered from the falling debris.

Nor did they have a plan and place to meet if they were separated, and in their search for loved ones they made an inventory of signs—black tarps hanging in the bare trees, a page from *The Sound and the Fury,* an affidavit from a case settled out of court, shards from the stained glass window of the church in which the steeple lies now in the nave—that no one could decipher.

While the newlyweds lingered over dinner, savoring the braised lamb shanks and *orzo* they had cooked for the first time and a Côtes du Rhône they could not afford, with the siren blaring above Dexter Gordon's *Go.*

But when their ears popped they rushed to the basement, refilled their glasses and, linking arms, toasted their luck, with hail clattering against the walls that soon gave way, trapping them in their embrace—which lasted until morning.

A night they would remember as the flurry of activity before a train arrives, and then the stillness after it departs.

———————

The old woman was lighting candles in the Tenebrae hearse, in a brick church about to be stripped of its icons and altar, pews and walls.

She could not imagine such a solemn service building to the great noise of sirens, with the wind extinguishing the candles, and then—nothing.

Nor the silence in which she wandered through the streets until she came to a house shorn of its façade, before which she stood, astonished.

Laid bare in the dining room were the secrets of a family torn asunder at their last meal together: a bottle of wine, a loaf of bread, a trunk of letters detailing another life.

Assuredly, I say to you, one of you will betray Me, Jesus told His disciples at table.

How to explain the darkness into which they had fallen, thanks to their heedlessness?

And if another covenant was inscribed in the tracks of the storm? Time to seek shelter.

Palm Sunday

I

Our last *mojito* in Havana was,
Of course, the best, because we were together,
Relaxing by the pool as the sun set
Over the palms, where I had sent our minder
To pick for you a bouquet of hibiscus—
A parting gift from the intelligence
Community, I joked, which had already
Given us more than we had bargained for:
Umbrellas for our walk one windy night
In the salt spray along the Malecón
(Cleared of the hookers who had propositioned us
The night before); a tour of the art school
And the Museum of the Revolution,
In the ballroom of which I should have taken
Your hand in mine and waltzed around the guards;
Interminable meetings with Fidel,
In which dear Gabo would doze off—a victim
Of the divine *mojito,* sacrificed
On the same altar as Papa Hemingway,
Whose limit was sixteen a day. Brave soul!
How quickly we learned to worship this concoction—
Club soda, rum, and syrup, with some sprigs
Of mint, a wedge of lime, and enough ice,
Our minder liked to say, to break the fever
Of the ruling class. He was a bookish spook
Who had in his collection first editions
Of *Harmonium* and *The Old Man and the Sea.*
Which may account for his ability
To anticipate each step of our affair
So that we learned much more about ourselves
Than what we were supposed to catalogue:

The island's crumbling infrastructure; the strength
Of the regime; the opposition's prospects . . .
In truth I was more interested in you
Than in the buildings falling into the sea—
You in your culottes and a halter top,
And me in my cream-colored linen suit
Stained at the collar. What a pair we made,
With a vintage Chevrolet at our disposal
And time enough, we thought, to fall in love,
If not to come up with a plausible
Explanation for the lapses in our report.
And while inventing stories for our spouses
Was not a problem—we were, after all,
Experienced travelers—nevertheless
We soon began to suffer from the vague
Dissatisfaction that shoddy work provokes.
Thus our private joke—*so much to see,
So little time to spend in bed*—wore thin
Before we gauged the depth of our discontent
And turned against our minder. *Gracias, amigo!*
If only he had stayed away for good.

II

It was on Palm Sunday, a sweltering,
Overcast morning when my head was pounding
From an excess of rum, that I realized
What we had missed in our mindless cavorting
From one expensive, wire-tapped suite to another:
The daily lives of men and women caught
In history's nets. The colorful procession
To the cathedral, with the faithful waving
Above their heads small blue-and-white striped flags,
Which fluttered like the wings of butterflies
(Recorded by our friends and foes alike),

Recalled us to the spirit of our mission.
It was the kind of detail that no one
Could invent, like the fight between the poet
And the novelist, which in the masterful
Retelling of our host (Gabo had a knack
For waking at the moment when Fidel
Needed a story to deflect his anger
At the line of questioning we were pursuing)
Pitted the courtly Stevens drunkenly
Punching the heavyweight—and breaking his wrist.
How to explain *that* to his wife? He told her
That he had fallen down a flight of stairs—
A sad invention that inspired our host
To improvise a scene in which the poet
Was in a batting cage, in a tuxedo
In Old Havana, flailing at a fastball
That any fool could hit. *Strike!* cried Fidel.
A senior advisor bolted out the door.
Our minder signaled to us: no sudden moves.
And while we were imagining the worst
Gabo ordered another round of drinks,
And asked Fidel whether he would have pitched
Around DiMaggio—which launched, alas,
Another monologue about the evil
Empire, with detours through his changing views
On civil and guerrilla war; the connection
Between madness and sugar-cane production;
The sexual prowess of the rum-runners;
The greenness of the grass in Yankee Stadium
(How it was fertilized by the bone marrow
Of the outfielders buried there); the glamour
Of Marilyn Monroe; the perfidy
Of the translators at the United Nations,
And so on until dawn . . . My notes are blurred.
The poet had the final word, however,
On the dictator and his associates,

Singing beyond the mandate of his time—
The history of which commenced, he thought,
With a rabbi entering Jerusalem
Atop a donkey and ended in a cloud
Of ashes and debris at Hiroshima.
And since the imagination was his theme,
Its healing properties and propositions
About time, space, and the uncharted regions
Of the believing heart, I am compelled
To celebrate its role in this fantasia
About two human rights *provocateurs,*
Two lonely unbelievers in Havana
Consistently misreading what was there
For anyone to see: the final credits
Unrolling on a film that no one liked,
With a nostalgic score arranged for strings
And oboe and conducted by a loyal
Son of the proletariat. *Encore,*
No one (save apparatchiks) was crying then.
Logical lunatics: this was the name
The poet gave to revolutionaries,
To the single-minded in a plural world.
He might have said the same of you and me.

III

After the final no: this was our minder's
Standard reply to our requests to meet
With dissidents, inspect the prisons, or visit
An NGO in the interior—
Which we had learned about from his own wife,
A disillusioned dancer who had given
Her knees and eyesight to the revolution.
She wore fatigues on stage, and smoked cigars
Wrapped in the pages of *Das Kapital,*

And hated her obsession with Fidel.
Her husband's fawning manner toward us
Inspired her to describe the charity
Run by a Jesuit expelled from his order—
Because of his excessive zeal, she explained.
He preached the Gospel in the guise of holding
The government to the ideals set forth
In the first heady days of the insurrection.
She took us to the station after dinner,
Navigating the dark streets and the ferry,
Then finding seats for us over the objections
Of the conductor planted in the aisle.
And who can blame her if the engineer
Uncoupled our car from the train at midnight
To leave us sweating far from the next town?
It was as though the other passengers
Expected this: they forced the windows open
To let in air, and made a meal of bread
And bottles of warm beer, then went to sleep.
In retrospect, our spat over the merits
Of your insect repellent versus mine,
Which was not lost on the tobacco picker
Who woke to stare at us, marked our return
To a professional relationship.
I was, in short, relieved to see you fall
Asleep (although the tobacco picker kept
An eye on you until I shook my fist
At him). And with mosquitoes hovering
Above your lips, while from the dark beyond
The window palm fronds crashed to the forest floor,
I meditated on the difficulties
Of breaking off any entanglement—
In love and faith, in ideology
And war—before returning to the theme
Of speaking truth to power, the idea
That every tyranny produces men

And women unafraid to risk their lives
In order to preserve the liberties
Essential to a just society,
As when a cancer creates antibodies:
Hard to say which will prevail—the brave
Or the inert. For it was this idea
That drew us to our work, and to each other,
Although, admittedly, your bravery
Meant less to me than your long legs and your ass.
Still to articulate the stakes involved
In seeking out the truth and proclaiming it—
This was our bond. No doubt the Jesuit
Would have inspired us with his fearlessness;
And as the night wore on I understood
That we had missed our chance to be instructed
In the high art of courage; that we would
Return to our old lives, lit by a passion
That had propelled us past the scenes of grief
And misery we should have documented
For our unreliable paymasters; and that
We would not meet again. There was no need
To castigate our minder for his joke—
Stranding us in the jungle for the night—
Or even to mention it in our report,
Since I have recorded it in my Book of Hours,
Which is devoted to imagining
Another life—in which, of course, you figure
Prominently. *After the final no,*
The poet said, meaning, perhaps, the death
Of God, which spurred him to believe in what
He called the supreme fiction, refreshing life
With hoobla-hows and syllables of salt.
His words, refracted through our minder's lens,
Revealed new meaning for me on the train,
For all at once I found myself in prayer,
Petitioning the Savior. Did he view

His last Passover as the final no?
Did He foresee the night of prayer, the kiss
And the betrayal, the trial, the crown of thorns,
The long walk up the hill, the guards, the weeping
Women, the vinegary sponge, the spear,
The earthquake and eclipse and empty tomb?
I watched you sleep, and wondered why we had
Neglected to consider dissidence
From a religious angle: if the Messiah
Was the embodiment of truth, then surely
The faithful marching in Havana knew
The way the verse would end: *there comes a yes* . . .
I would hold you in my arms until you woke.

Paschal Stanzas

Haunted by the procession, the voice instructor
Was harping on about the stained glass windows
Cracked during the liturgy, when a grenade
Struck the façade of the historic church.
He ordered the ventriloquists to leave.
He cast his voices at the Crucifixion
Splintering in the nave: *Thy kingdom come* . . .
And then he retreated to the catacombs.

––––––––––

When God changed Abram's name to Abraham,
Promising him increase of kings and nations,
Faith gained a new dimension: a covenant—
From *Here am I* to *Where are you?*—and a chasm
To bridge through prayer. Thus the prophecy:
A nervous governor in the final days
Of his campaign on terror will read aloud
The names of the condemned: Barrabas, Jesus . . .

––––––––––

And when He said the Jews *would do the works*
Of Abraham, if they were not intent
Upon delivering Him up to the Romans,
His subject was the servitude of sin
And the necessity of discovering
Freedom in God, abiding in His Word.
And now? If only I could break the habit
Of hiding myself from the face of love.

Christopher

The child grew heavier and heavier
Until we were halfway across the river,
And then he said, "Do you know who I am?"
Yes. And He was light as the fleece of a lamb.

Trinity

for the sesquicentennial celebration of
Trinity Church, Iowa City, Iowa

I

From a seam pressed deep in the earth, below a drift of blue clay and a peat bog sealed in during the last ice age, a sliver of petrified moss: an ancient specimen of the first plants to cover the trees and walls of Eden. Someone gave it to the bishop visiting the frontier, the missionary who dreamed of a church—a prairie ark. And so in a gothic steamboat, set on a hill above the river, in flood and drought, in wind and war, the ceremonies are performed, the faithful sing hosannas, the figures in the stained glass windows brighten and darken with the seasons of sowing and harvest and rest. The moss? In a petri dish it divides into russet stems with tufts as delicate as the scales on a butterfly's wing; in water they wriggle away, like tadpoles. Something remains—splinters of the True Cross: *If you have faith as a mustard seed, you can say to this mulberry tree, "Be pulled up by the roots and be planted in the sea," and it would obey you.*

II

When the bishops gathered in Nicea
To condemn the heresy of Arius
(Christ is man, not God, the sailors sang)
And write the creed that unified the empire,
Saint Antony, physician of all Egypt,
Prayed with his brethren in a cave, chanting
Psalms through the desert night: *Holy, holy, holy.*

And when the Crusaders sacked Constantinople,
Killing and pillaging, burning books and inspiring
The approaching infidels to greater savagery,

A hermit on the Holy Mountain tied a rope
Around his waist and, leaning over a cliff
Hundreds of feet above the sea, praised God
Daylong, nightlong, until his final hour.

And when the island church annulled the marriage
Of the queen consort (she had not produced
An heir, she must be an adulterer,
Off with her head), a poet who had loved her
Fashioned out of words a net to catch
The wind that splintered the alliance of popes and kings—
The breath, love, faith: *three persons in one essence.*

III

What they saw in prayer on the mountain—His garments as white as
snow, His face shining like the sun—was light: the divine radiance in
which God first spoke to Moses and the prophets.

And now the Lawgiver was talking with Elijah and the Messiah, backlit by
the cloud in which God spoke for the last time: *This is my beloved Son, in
whom I am well pleased. Hear Him!*

Centuries passed, during which the three tabernacles the disciple offered
to make for the holy men were united in the doctrine of the Trinity; the
Church grew, divided, splintered; and one day Saint Gregory of Sinai drew
a map of the mind—intellect, consciousness, spirit—corresponding to
the Godhead, a map still accurate in every detail.

Triangles, triads, tercets. How to account for this need to order experi-
ence in threes? The sonata. Dialectical reasoning. Past, present, future.
Even if the image of the three figures on the mountain no longer struc-
tures the search for meaning—triptychs, trilogies, *the third time is the
charm*—the faithful learn to heed every beginning, middle, and end.

And if a butterfly flapping its wings in the Amazon rain forest causes winds to gather in the Gobi desert, then surely the prayers rising from the church on the hill register in the currents and swells of the sea the solitary mariner crosses at night.

The spring peepers cling to the leaves of the trees surrounding the pond, filling the woods at dusk with cries of longing, which drift through the air, like pollen. New life, new life! This is what we hear at Easter, when we walk the fields prepared for planting.

Forgive us if the sleep of the disciples through the revelation of the Lord's exodus from Jerusalem comes over us even as we murmur, *Father, Son, and Holy Ghost.*

Stanzas on the Joy of Faith

The rabbit feeding on the lettuces
Vanished from the last page of a book
Expertly sliced up with a pair of scissors
By the lost boy whose father never took
The time to teach him how to throw a ball
To the angel always at his beck and call.

––––––––––

The prophet said: *Grief mingles not with mirth.*
But here below I heard a man accused
Of slashing a painting of the Virgin's Birth
Ask to be sentenced to twelve lashes. Bruised
And buoyant, he sashayed through the prison yard
As if he had been granted a vision of God.

––––––––––

What do you think that naughty rabbit's doing?
The woman asked the girl in the last row
Of the airplane. The child said, *I don't know,*
And counted, through the window, bolts of lightning
In the night sky. *Don't panic,* said her mother.
We're above the storm. And so they were.

IV

Vast

Steppe, desert, sea: to seek the vast *not as a grudging obligation* but to honor what cannot be measured or imagined in its full dimensions. Emptiness, not desolation. God's essence *and* His energies, everywhere hidden—and everywhere revealed. Thus the newlyweds camping at the confluence of two rivers were awakened one night by a geology student whose friends had hiked into a canyon and never returned. Half-asleep, crawling out of their tent, they saw the stars, the shadows on the rock formations, and their gooseflesh as emblems of another order, like the smell of sage on the drive to the visitors' center, the map on which the park ranger traced the students' possible routes, the decision to wait until first light to send a search party. The trail was too steep to navigate in the dark. This, too, would mark their marriage.

A handful of coal dust blown from an open railroad car on the Asian steppe, mixed with loess and borne aloft across the Pacific, settled in an orchard on the edge of the Russian River, into which it flowed in the spring runoff, through the valleys, vineyards, and redwood forests of Mendocino and Sonoma, through the days and nights of families in crisis and at peace, until it emptied into the ocean, in a hamlet called Jenner by the Sea, where the waves roll into the bay and crash against the rocks, and the salt spray glimmers at Blind Beach, and a hawk rising on an updraft tastes something new.

Where's the zoom? said the guide, fumbling with a camera focused on the haunches of a young woman who wanted a record of her camel ride in the Gobi desert. The sun burned through her straw hat and glint-ed off the aluminum saucers on the crest of the dune rising above her, where children awaited their turn to coast downhill. Oh, for a tall glass of water, thought the guide, unable to switch off the camera or to change its focus—which, if he were to be honest with himself, was exactly where he wanted it to be. The woman shifted her weight. The camel took a step. A boy sailed through the sky.

The juvenile sandbar shark trapped and thrashing in the ebbing tide, in the seawrack and clack of water rushing over stones and shells, in the murmuring of the sunbathers and fishermen attracted to its dorsal fins, cannot save itself from the air and the morning sun; and so it wriggles in the foam, yearning for the shallows in which it fed all night on squid and minnows, for the tidal sway and measure of the full moon that lit the depths, for the wave that gathered speed off the continental shelf, bending the seaweed and strands of kelp, and cast it ashore on this barrier island, the shifting contours of which are subject to the winds, budgetary whims of legislators, and decisions taken by the dredger working his way toward the inlet, replenishing the beach with sand.

According to the legend of the Pulpit Rock, if seven brothers marry seven sisters from the same fjord the flat square slab of granite looming over the narrow inlet will shear off the cliff and crash into the water, triggering a tidal wave tall enough to clear the coast. And in the myth of perpetual happiness a bored couple set sail for the Faroe Islands to save their marriage, discovering not *a floating fortress* but fog and wind, dried mutton and whale meat—sagas of daily life, with the sea rising all around them, the young leaving for the mainland, the steps to the chain dance receding in memory. And who can blame them for wishing to distill into a single line a history of their time here below; to write an equation with which to light the darkness; to chart a new course to the origin?

In the beginning . . . That a narrative of the unbidden should derive from nothingness, from the vast, from the workings of the divine on the things of the earth—sunlight on water, moonlight on water. That the unnamed be entered in a ledger of desire, along with all the words for failure. That the unseen bends us toward the light, the way a lily opening at daybreak follows the course of the sun toward the horizon.

That night they were undressing by the river, under a canyon wall streaked with desert varnish and petroglyphs, when an airplane stalled overhead and glided soundlessly out of sight. And they gave themselves to each other in the spirit of the flute player etched into the rock, while the passengers stared out their windows. One cried that they were going to die, another scribbled a note to his family and tucked it in his wallet, a third began to sing. The lovers, collapsing in the sand, heard the ruffle of wings on water. *What a strange light,* they said at the same moment, and their laughter stirred the land. They traced their fingers over their fevered lips, imagining the future as a series of adventures cloaked in mystery. And if they were asleep when the search party fanned out across the desert, heading for the debris field? Sweet dreams.

Ghazal

for Agha Shahid Ali (1949–2001)

There's no sugar in the Promised Land.
Swear by the olive in the God-kissed land.

I heard your laughter in the jackal's howl
When the monks chanted in the Psalmist's land.

They knelt on the mountaintop, pilgrims of the Book,
Until the viper in the rod hissed, "Stand!"

Prophets, oracles, and bards agree:
The tyrant always plays the dumbest hand.

The way you danced along the crowded bar—
The saffron harvest in a star-crossed land.

Our teacher, moon-tanned, slept with one eye open.
He was *the absence of field,* the sodless strand.

The faithful praying in the catacombs—
Do they measure what they must withstand?

These orders from Iberia remain
In effect: *Like unto like. All others banned.*

They set sail without charts or compass, searching
For the lost tribes, and never missed land.

Lava and salt spray and your final couplet:
New worlds inscribed in parchment, pumice, sand.

The cemeteries above Sarajevo
Extend the boundaries of a lost land.

Your favorite show: *General Hospital.*
Shall we go for a walk? No! I'll get tanned.

In Beirut, Baghdad, and Jerusalem
The war photographers are in command.

The heart turned terrorist when the poet died.
Now all the world's a revolutionist land.

If Paradise is full of stationery, write
To me in your most lavish, embossed hand.

Eat seven olives, my grandmother said,
And you will never live in a famished land.

Another war in the imperium?
The poet's warnings can be read, glossed, scanned.

Unwitnessed in the night, the empty mosques
And temples burn in the Belovéd's land.

The new exhibit in the war museum—
Portraits commissioned in a possessed land.

Ragas at daybreak, Motown at midnight:
You sang for everyone, a wind-tossed band.

Will this Christ-bearer find his only friend
In the Promised Land—in blesséd Shahid's land?

S. Diwakar: *The World*

A novelist writes about another novelist who is writing two novels about
two other novelists, one writing novels to tell lies, the other to search
for truth. In the 42 novels about 42 novelists they write, there are some
novelists completely unaware of the lies they tell or deliberately telling
lies or some who look for truth knowing pretty well they won't find it or
some skeptical about the truth they find. And those 47 novelists write 560
novels describing 1,585 novelists, and among those 1,585 novelists, while
some novelists behave childishly even after having grown old in dozens
of novels, others (some of them women) hang on to some ideals because
of their Western education, and, despite marriage and family worries,
become social reformers in about 60 novels, yet others rebel for reasons
of their ideals or nation or selfishness and start a revolution against pov-
erty and inequality in 920 novels, and only one novelist, leaving his home
and family and traveling around the country, fights for the freedom of
his nation and writes a beautiful novel about another novelist who, like
himself, leaving his home and family to travel around the country, fights
for the freedom of his nation, and finally gets killed. The main character
of another novel about another novelist, a person from the same town as
that of the dead novelist, suffers from loneliness even while stressing the
need for subjectivity, forgets the very existence of the dead novelist and
writes a novel about 2,088 novelists who in turn write 5,831 novels nar-
rating the eternal plight of society's oppressed peoples and 3,216 novels
depicting the interior landscapes of women. In 9,057 novels those 2,088
novelists write there appear 13,702 novelists whose 20,829 novels tell the
story of only one novelist who, although he tries to write a single novel
about one other novelist, fails to complete that novel, meets the other
novelist and, to kill him, boils down all the novelists, including himself,
numbering 13,701, 9,057, 2,088, 1,585, 47, 2, 1, and finally becomes the
single novelist known as the novelist of all novelists.

—translated from the Kannada with the author

Coordinates

A map on which the names have been erased,
A compass pivoting on a black cross,
Sextants dismantled and displayed in a store
Razed and rebuilt in the Jewish Quarter—this is
How to draw coordinates for the next battle
On memory and desire, with a set of tools
No one knows how to use. And so the colonel
Peeling an orange at the command post
Hums an aria from *La Bohème*
Until a mortar lands outside his door.

———————

The trial will resume next week, if the judge
Survives the latest attempt on his life, though the jury
Impaneled for the duration of the war
Cannot reach a verdict in the case
Of the man gagged and hanging from the ceiling
Of the machine shop: the ghost prisoner,
AKA God's beloved. His testimony
Must be thrown out, new witnesses examined,
And the court reporters banished before the judge
Can order him to be strung up again.

———————

Cicadas emerge, numbered and ranked, their clear
Wings beating—a light arriving from a star
Glimpsed from the depths of an abandoned mine.
We won't make it out alive, the guide said
And tumbled down the shaft. What remains?
A shred of plastic flapping in the nest

The birds left in the hedge, a speckled egg
That never hatched, a file of summonses
Lost in the flood. The trees hum in the dark.
Pray for the guide. Pray for everyone.

———————

Heroic poses generate suspicion,
According to a poll taken on board
The wooden ship bound for the Orient.
Hence the captain's orders are delivered
Through the sous-chef who signed up to resurrect
The art of navigating by the stars.
The first mate is afraid to leave his cabin.
The stowaway will lead the mutineers.
And the passengers will tell you anything
If you will take them safely to Ceylon.

———————

To break the back of the iambic line,
The prisoner in his metal cage, exposed
To sun and wind and rain, summoned a host
Of voices from the vast storehouse of his reading
And listening, and cast them on the page
Like glittering shells collected at high tide,
In a new line variable as the surf
He could no longer hear from his death cell
In Pisa: *by the law, so build yr/ temple* . . .
The verdict? Silence and unsentencing.

———————

The tower leans toward mystery. Which is to say:
The past, present, and future, the masonry
Of which is lined with cracks through which to glimpse

A second space—i.e., eternity.
Thus Mimi, coughing, seizes Rodolfo's sleeve
To sing goodbye. Thus a seasick passenger
Prays for deliverance. And thus the poet charged
With treason marks off in the sand the days
Until his execution, while the colonel
Is buried with full military honors.

After the torture and interrogations,
The water-boarding and sleep deprivation
And menstrual blood flung in his face, the ghost
Prisoner revealed the coordinates
For the Roman razing of Jerusalem
And the itinerary that John followed
To Patmos to compose his Revelation
For the seven churches in Asia. The guard
Removed her underwear. *And from the throne
Proceeded lightnings, thunderings, and voices . . .*

The Petitions

The edifice was complete—the signatures, secret teachings, and sacrificial victims locked in stone, the jewelry, linens, and banners of the vanquished hung from the parapets—when a great wind swept through the city.

The walls and towers glistened with salt spray; a sheet of music sailed down the street, toward the harbor, where the last fishing trawler was in flames; the door to the lighthouse swung open; no one entered or left.

The harbor was protected by a natural lagoon, beyond which sailed a fleet of warships, of indeterminate origin, awaiting the order to attack.

An order that would be delivered from on high, said the trusted courtiers.

Pearl divers, purse seiners, silk traders, coffee merchants, vendors, vintners, customs officers, carvers of casks, gunrunners, sawyers, salt collectors, street cleaners, appraisers and collectors, surveyors and adjusters—all fled with their families.

The city they built in the desert grew concentrically, adding rings of houses and roads that reached into the mountains, where a band of anchorites had settled to await the end of time, keeping vigil through the day and night.

Do not be foolish in your petitions, one monk advised his brethren, *lest you dishonor God by your ignorance*—and still they begged for more: miracles and visions and glory.

Of Whom they knew nothing, for all their certainty about the intricacies of His design.

The same certainty that governed the spread of the city to the edge of the known world.

Beyond the border, refugees from the flood plain huddled around fires fed by the timbers of the boats swamped in the storm that washed their huts and horses away.

The faithful watched this spectacle as if from a great distance, conscious of the fact that disaster is always near at hand.

Praying to be spared: *Lord, have mercy . . .*

Suite for Ashes and Strings

The last composer in the labor camp
Wrote chamber music for the prisoners
To play until the conquering army arrived
To count the dead and bury them in mounds
Along the river—levees to protect
The fields of the peasant who supplied the guards
With grain, girls, and the names of all the partisans
In the surrounding hills and villages—
And so the tempo changes in every measure
From light to darkness, water to rock: *One, two* . . .

————————

The chemist tips a beaker toward the flame,
The cantor in the ruins of a church
Chants to the birds, and a seam opening
In the mountain connects a funnel in the clouds
To the ensemble of official voices
Restricted to the garden: the courtier
Who monitors the pulse of the waterfall,
The scribe who records the size of the pomegranate,
The spokesman who cannot explain the cries
Of the envoy rising from the patio . . .

————————

The lake is burning, and the angels wave
At the crowd gathering on the shore. Above
The trees, in the grey vault of the sky, the last
Light is locked away. An empty nest
Flutters to the ground. The sleeveless ones,

The men with marching orders and the women
Wading up to their necks, laugh at the tyrant's joke:
The box of broken treaties for the birthday
Of his foreign minister. The angels sing
Through the smoke and ash. The tyrant seals the scrolls . . .

Bill

for William Matthews (1942–1997)

As in a statement of particulars:
A drooping mustache and an aching hip;
A penchant for *bons mots* and rumpled shirts;
A standup tragic, as he liked to say.
Dead at the age . . . The author of . . . Survived by . . .

As in to issue or announce, to touch
And rub, to caress: women, words *(good, bad,
Right, wrong),* a glass of wine. Another glass?
Don't mind if I do. And then the lights
Went out, and so we never saw the end

Of the empire, a novel might begin,
In which the solos of his stand-in, a blind
Jazz drummer hopelessly in love with smoky
Bars and the rhythms of America,
Separate light from dark, the wheat from the chaff.

As in a formal petition *(obsolete):*
To language, say, or to the gods of misrule,
Time, and desire, which coaxed from him a blues,
A body of work to replace his own
Stiff joints and remorse, revising, then revised.

As in the jaws of the peregrine falcon,
The "cosmopolitan" perched on the skyscraper;
The point of an anchor digging into sand;
The visor of a baseball cap. As in
The check. Check, please. The tip's included. Thank you.

Music Lessons

Carved out of cherry wood, with a black rubber
Mouthpiece and keys that stick, this clarinet
Was passed from one child to another, like a cold.
No one could play in tune. And no one cared
Except the band teacher who needed winds
To balance the percussion and the brass—
The instruments of choice for the boys in his class.

And so the boy who wanted to play drums
Would suck on his reeds until they split, adjust
The joints to no effect, and inspect the worn
Pads on the keys, like moleskin around a blister,
Delaying the inevitable lesson,
Of which he would remember nothing beyond
The teacher's aggravation at his sound,

His lapses in rhythm, his awkward fingerings.
If only you would practice! His favorite thing?
To pull the swab from the barrel to the bell,
Soaking up his saliva, then look inside,
As if to clean the bore of the .22
Locked in the gun case. O what did he ever hear,
Aiming his clarinet at the chandelier?

Ghazal (2)

for Dawn Upshaw

O water, be the string to my guitar.
The land's encircled? Follow the evening star.

The flight attendant heads for her hotel—
The fossil of a bird rising through the tar.

Another photo shoot for the pregnant model
We met in Andalusia, in a bar!

The way the sun burned through the morning fog—
Blood from a white-tailed deer struck by a car.

The soldier at the checkpoint waved us through,
While the mendicant examined his cigar.

A plague of locusts and a partial eclipse
Of the sun: send a virgin to the altar.

The neurologist at his retirement party
Thanked everyone for gauging him from afar.

The sun, the mountains, and the sea: these framed
The tragedy born of the scimitar.

Bored? Seeking love? Adventure? The divine?
It's a good time to go to Zanzibar.

The emperor dismissed the courtier
Who had prepared for famine instead of war.

And so they charged into an ancient land,
Like cattle herded into an abattoir.

The scholar's parting gift to the defrocked priest:
The fetus of an ape, preserved in a jar.

Take the reins, please. Now. I can't see the road,
Thanks to the blows I received from that hussar.

The naturalist bitten by a rattlesnake
Wore a black leather glove to hide his scar.

Steer clear of the volcano rising from the sea
Or else you'll lose that load of cinnebar.

They entertained the spirits of their marriage—
A turning of the bones in Madagascar.

A plume of smoke and ashes on the deck.
The startled lookout dangles from the spar.

Again they rose at dawn to sing hosannas:
If you're a Romanov, then I'm the czar.

West Window

for W. S. Merwin

Green as the palm that fans the hill and hides
Flames at its base, the lizard slides or falls
From frond to flower, a raindrop disappearing
Into the ferns below. The island's mimics—
Mynas and mockingbirds—sing when the cardinal
Flies from the hutch to the mango and beyond.
The bamboo creaks. Doors open. No one's home.

———————

The cardinal preening   in the palm transplanted
from Indonesia   is not the island's
sentry nor the sea's   ambassador
winds waves and wings   whirl at the sound of the last
door closing   in the leper colony
below the bluff   where the *brilliant water* is
wearing down the wreckage   from the war

———————

The dying man was still drawing up plans, this time for a prison. Candles flickered, and outside his window songbirds fell like rain; choristers trapped them in the cisterns to roast over a spit. A priest opened a book and recorded the statesman's final words: *Who are the enemies of France? The German princes? Their lands are burning. The Holy Roman Empire is a leper colony. Open the window on the West. We shall leave seeds and feathers everywhere.* The Master of Royal Fireworks was in the courtyard, tasting sauces for the songbirds. Courtesans poured wine for the choristers. *The blows from a sword are easily healed. Not so the blows of a tongue* . . . The priest scribbled in the margins: *Delirium has set in.* Fireworks rained down on the city, like songbirds.

The cisterns were filled with burning oil. Soon the swollen empire would split in two. Lepers were at the door. But just before he closed his eyes the cardinal heard the poet's voice: *Where are the snows of yesteryear?* And that is why it is said that he died peacefully in his sleep.

Salt

The rescue gear? It was like finding salt
Under the floorboards of a burning house,
Barrels of salt from the sea. For we believed
The flames resembled migrants in a field
Scattering at the sputter of the plane
That spilled white dust over the twisted vines.
A woman hid her children under her skirt;
An old man climbed a tree, without a noose;
The plane swept back and forth until the air
Was whiter than the church—*Our father who . . .*

Knife, matches, map; a Psalter, not a flare;
A blanket and a rope—*What shall we do?*
It was like boiling water in a wound.
Salt it, salt it! The house was burning down,
The plane would never stall. And who would grieve?
The dirt was sweet, and the children didn't cry
Or crawl away. The old man shook the tree
Until the leaves were nooses and the church
Was full. The field was hallowed, like the sea.

So wrap the children in the blanket, salt
The old man's wound, and let the woman sleep
Under the tree that never grows or sways.
The sea is in the barrel, and the house
Is filled with ashes whiter than the dove
That flew inside the church. It burned for days,
The dusted field. The rope was long enough
To teach us how to grieve: call it a map.
The plane was flying higher than the flames.
So light another flare—*and thy will be done . . .*

Vespers

The hammer falls silent, a mourning dove coos in the pigeon house by the olive grove, and in the renovated church the bells ring for vespers.

I close the illustrated Book of the Sea to read from a pocket-sized manual of prayers, trading soundings and silhouettes of headlands for another anchorage:

Now that the day hath run its course, I praise thee, O Holy One . . .

And if my petitions for favor lead to an examination of the soul?

Forty years ago, boarding a sailboat, I saw my father wind his watch around his wallet, a stripe of gold cinching a wad of leather, like an amulet.

And when the mast snapped in a gust of wind, capsizing the boat, his watch and wallet sank to the bottom of the lake.

What I remember from underwater were the bubbles of my breath rising to the surface, the taste of algae, the greenish tinge of the sun and sky.

Thus a life of pure sensation passed before my eyes—and little has changed since then.

Time and money, my father joked, rowing back to shore.

To which I add: *Into thy hands, O Lord Jesus Christ, my God, I commend my spirit . . .*

Acknowledgments

"Ark" was commissioned by the choreographer Charlotte Adams for *Dance Gala 2004.*

"Trinity" was commissioned by Trinity Episcopal Church, Iowa City, Iowa, to celebrate the 150th anniversary of its founding.

"Valves" was commissioned for the installation of David Skorton as the nineteenth president of the University of Iowa.

"The Ideal Reader," "Trinity," and "Valves" appeared in broadsides made by Shari DeGraw.

"Bill" was first published in *Blues for Bill: A Tribute to William Matthews,* edited by Kurt Brown, Meg Kearney, Donna Resi, and Estha Weiner (University of Akron Press, 2005), and also included in *Under the Rock Umbrella: Contemporary American Poets from 1951–1977,* edited by William Walsh (Mercer University Press, 2006), along with "Suite for Ashes and Strings."

"The Ground Swell" was first published in *A Mingling of Waters: A Commemorative Program,* edited by Catherine Fletcher (Supernova P & D, 2008).

"West Window," which first appeared in *Notre Dame Review,* was reprinted in *Notre Dame Review: The First Ten Years,* edited by John Matthias and William O'Rourke (Notre Dame University Press, 2008).

I am grateful to the editors of the following publications, in which some of these poems and translations first appeared, sometimes in different versions: *Atlas@las, The Café Review. The Cream City Review, Cyphers, The Huffington Post, Iowa Review, Mānoa, Modern Poetry in Translation, Notre Dame Review, Poetry Northwest, Seattle Review, 66: The Journal of Sonnet Studies, tin lustre mobile,* and *Words Without Borders.*

My thanks to Bruce Rogers, Patricia Caswell, and their staff at the Hermitage Artist Retreat, where *Boat* was assembled, and to Barbara Ras, Barry Sanders, Jim Schley, and David St. John for their close reading of this book, wise editorial suggestions, and enduring friendship.

Other Books from Tupelo Press

Fasting for Ramadan: Notes from a Spiritual Practice (memoir), Kazim Ali
This Lamentable City (poems), Polina Barskova,
    edited and introduced by Ilya Kaminsky
Circle's Apprentice (poems), Dan Beachy-Quick
The Vital System (poems), CM Burroughs
Stone Lyre: Poems of René Char, translated by Nancy Naomi Carlson
Severance Songs (poems), Joshua Corey
Atlas Hour (poems), Carol Ann Davis
New Cathay: Contemporary Chinese Poetry, edited by Ming Di
Sanderlings (poems), Geri Doran
The Flight Cage (poems), Rebecca Dunham
The Posthumous Affair (novel), James Friel
Nothing Can Make Me Do This (novel), David Huddle
Meridian (poems), Kathleen Jesme
Darktown Follies (poems), Amaud Jamaul Johnson
Dancing in Odessa (poems), Ilya Kaminsky
A God in the House: Poets Talk About Faith (interviews),
    edited by Ilya Kaminsky and Katherine Towler
Manoleria (poems), Daniel Khalastchi
domina Un/blued (poems), Ruth Ellen Kocher
Phyla of Joy (poems), Karen An-hwei Lee
Engraved (poems), Anna George Meek
Body Thesaurus (poems), Jennifer Militello
Mary & the Giant Mechanism (poems), Mary Molinary
After Urgency (poems), Rusty Morrison
Lucky Fish (poems), Aimee Nezhukumatathil
Long Division (poems), Alan Michael Parker
Ex-Voto (poems), Adélia Prado, translated by Ellen Doré Watson
Intimate: An American Family Photo Album (memoir), Paisley Rekdal
Thrill-Bent (novel), Jan Richman
Calendars of Fire (poems), Lee Sharkey
Cream of Kohlrabi: Stories, Floyd Skloot
The Perfect Life (essays), Peter Stitt
Swallowing the Sea (essays), Lee Upton
Butch Geography (poems), Stacey Waite
Dogged Hearts (poems), Ellen Doré Watson

See our complete backlist at www.tupelopress.org